THINGS
WITH
WINGS

# Bugs
## in Flight

Frankie Stout

**PowerKiDS** press.

New York

*To Mercedes, Terri, and everyone at the Woodbridge Animal Group. Thanks for all your work.*

Published in 2009 by The Rosen Publishing Group, Inc.
29 East 21st Street, New York, NY 10010

First Edition

Editor: Nicole Pristash
Book Design: Kate Laczynski
Photo Researcher: Jessica Gerweck

Photo Credits: Cover, p. 1 © Age fotostock.com; pp. 5, 7, 9, 11, 13, 15, 17, 19, 21 Shutterstock.com.

Library of Congress Cataloging-in-Publication Data

Stout, Frankie.
  Bugs in flight / Frankie Stout. — 1st ed.
      p. cm. — (Things with wings)
  Includes index.
  ISBN 978-1-4042-4493-1 (library binding)
  1. Insects—Juvenile literature. 2. Wings—Juvenile literature.  I. Title.
  QL467.2.S83 2009
  595.7'1479—dc22

                                                    2008000999


Manufactured in the United States of America

# CONTENTS

Bugs with Wings.................................................................4

Hide and Seek ..................................................................6

Baby Fliers ......................................................................8

All Abuzz.........................................................................10

Honeybees at Work ..........................................................12

A Hop and a Chirp ...........................................................14

Winged Rainbows ............................................................16

Presenting the Beetles! ....................................................18

Wet Bugs, Dry Bugs .........................................................20

What's So Great About Bugs with Wings? ..............22

Glossary..........................................................................23

Index ..............................................................................24

Web Sites ........................................................................24

# Bugs with Wings

Do you know what bugs are? Bugs are also called insects. You can find them everywhere. Some insects walk and some crawl. Some insects even bite and **sting**. It is fun to look at bugs and wonder what it would be like if you were a bug.

Most bugs have wings, and they use them to fly and to go from place to place. Some wings are clear. Other bugs' wings have bright colors. Most kinds of bugs have four wings, but some have only two. Let's look at some bugs that have interesting wings and find out how the bugs use them!

This interesting red insect is a dragonfly. Dragonflies are known for their beautiful and brightly colored wings.

5

# Hide and Seek

One kind of bug with cool wings is the butterfly. You can tell what kind of butterfly a certain butterfly is by looking at its wings. The leaf-wing butterfly has wings that look like leaves. This helps the butterfly **blend in** with real leaves. Its wings make the butterfly hard to see, so **predators** cannot find it.

Another butterfly with interesting wings is the buckeye. Buckeyes have wings with spots that look like eyes. When a predator sees the spots, the predator thinks the spots are the eyes of a larger animal. Their wings help keep these butterflies from being eaten!

This butterfly has spots on its wings, called eyespots. Eyespots will help keep this butterfly safe from its predators.

# Baby Fliers

A butterfly's wings are also used to help make baby butterflies. **Male** butterflies have special **scent** parts on their wings. The scent helps **female** butterflies find the males when it is time to **mate**. Mating is how butterflies make eggs. These eggs then **hatch** into squirmy caterpillars.

Caterpillars do not have wings when they are born. When a caterpillar is ready to grow, it makes a shell around its body, called a chrysalis. The caterpillar then stays inside the shell for a while. When the caterpillar leaves, it has become a butterfly with beautiful new wings.

Here you can see a butterfly coming out of its chrysalis. Before becoming a butterfly, a caterpillar rests inside its chrysalis for a few days to many months without eating or drinking.

9

# All Abuzz

Bees are another type of bug that has cool wings. Bees are in the same family as ants and wasps. Many bees live alone. They build nests in the ground or in the stems of plants. Other bees, like the honeybee, live in colonies. Colonies are groups of many bees. Bees that live in colonies are also called **social** bees.

Social bees build their colonies in trees or in hives built by beekeepers. Beekeepers tend to the bees and gather honey from the hives. This is called bee culture. Beekeepers may use the honey they culture, or they may sell it to other people.

These bees are working on a honeycomb. A honeycomb is inside a beehive. This is where honeybees store their honey.

# Honeybees at Work

A honeybee's wings help it work. Honeybees fly around and gather flower **nectar**. Later, at the hive, the nectar gets turned into honey. The honeybees beat their wings, which make a blast of air. This air helps the honey lose water and get thicker. Eating honey gives bees a lot of **energy** for growing and flying.

When honeybees gather nectar, the bees also pick up flower **pollen** on their legs. The bees fly to other flowers and take this pollen with them. The flowers then use the pollen to make fruit and seeds. Honeybees use their wings for important work!

When a bee brings pollen on its legs to another flower, it is called pollination. The pollen will help the flower grow seeds. Those seeds turn into more flowers.

13

# A Hop and a Chirp

Grasshoppers and crickets are bugs that use their wings to make sounds. Grasshoppers make sounds by rubbing their front wings against their back legs, which are ribbed. As the wings rub against the ribs, the wings make a sound. This sound is made in much the same way that you make a sound by running a stick across a fence.

Crickets make sounds, too. They make sounds by rubbing their left wings against their right wings. You can hear crickets sometimes at night if you listen. You can sit at a window in summer and hear them chirping.

Female crickets cannot make sounds, only male crickets can. A cricket hears sounds by using its ears, which are on its front legs!

# Winged Rainbows

Dragonflies are bugs with pretty wings. Each dragonfly has four wings. As they fly around looking for food, dragonflies use their wings to **hover** like a helicopter. Then they take off very quickly, like an airplane. As a dragonfly darts around in the air, its wings appear iridescent. "Iridescent" means that you can see the colors of the rainbow flash in the dragonfly's wings.

Dragonflies like to live near water. Dragonfly babies, called nymphs, do not have wings. When the nymphs grow into adults, their new wings let them fly through the air and hunt for food.

Here you can see the colors purple and green flashing off this dragonfly's wings as it sits on a branch.

# Presenting the Beetles!

Beetles are bugs with important wings. Beetle wings are very unique, or special. Their wings are different from the wings of most other bugs.

Beetles have four wings, but they use only two wings to fly. A beetle's wings grow so that one pair of wings covers the other pair. The top pair of wings is harder than the pair underneath. The top pair forms a shell that covers the beetle. Beetles fly using the pair of wings that is under this shell. A beetle's wings not only let it fly, but they also keep it safe from predators.

This is a dogwood calligrapha beetle. Its top wings are lifting from its bottom wings so it can take off!

19

# Wet Bugs, Dry Bugs

Some beetles live in or near water. These beetles are called aquatic beetles. Some aquatic beetles can stay in the water for a long time. To breathe, they trap air in a bubble under their wings. They breathe the air until it runs out. Then the beetles come out of the water to get more air.

Other beetles have a hard time finding water. In the desert, where it is dry, some beetles use their wings to get water to drink. They gather dew on bumps on their wings. The dew then rolls off the wings into the beetle's mouth.

Most animals could not live in a dry, hot desert. However, this darkling beetle has learned how to stay safe in such a dangerous place.

# What's So Great About Bugs with Wings?

Bugs are everywhere, flying around. They come in all shapes and in many sizes. Some are pretty and some even look a little strange.

Some of the most interesting bugs have wings. These bugs use their wings for many different things. Bees help nature by bringing pollen from flower to flower. Beetles use their wings to keep themselves safe. Butterflies use their wings to stay alive and to make baby butterflies.

Bugs with wings are fun to watch. Next time you see some outside or in your backyard, take a closer look and see how cool they are!

**blend in** (BLEND IN)  To go unnoticed by looking or acting like something else.

**energy** (EH-nur-jee)  The power to work or to act.

**female** (FEE-mayl)  Having to do with women and girls.

**hatch** (HACH)  To come out of an egg.

**hover** (HUH-ver)  To fly in place in the air.

**male** (MAYL)  Having to do with men and boys.

**mate** (MAYT)  To come together to make babies.

**nectar** (NEK-tur)  A sweet liquid found in flowers.

**pollen** (PAH-lin)  A yellow dust made by the male parts of flowers.

**predators** (PREH-duh-terz)  Animals that kill other animals for food.

**scent** (SENT)  Something that is sensed by the nose.

**social** (SOH-shul)  Living together in a group.

**sting** (STING)  To cause pain using a sharp part of an animal's body.

**B**
bees, 10, 12, 22
buckeye(s), 6
butterfly, 6, 8, 22

**C**
caterpillars, 8
colors, 4, 16

**D**
dragonflies, 16

**E**
eggs, 8
energy, 12
eyes, 6

**I**
insects, 4

**L**
leaf-wing butterfly, 6
leaves, 6

**M**
males, 8

**N**
nectar, 12

**P**
pollen, 12, 22
predators, 6, 18

Due to the changing nature of Internet links, PowerKids Press has developed an online list of Web sites related to the subject of this book. This site is updated regularly. Please use this link to access the list:
www.powerkidslinks.com/wings/bugs/